Learn French

A beginner's guide to learning basic French fast, including useful common words and phrases!

Table Of Contents

Introduction	v
Chapter 1 – An Introduction to the French language	1
Chapter 2 – The French Alphabet, Accents, and Punctuation	5
Chapter 3 – Liaisons and Contractions	16
Chapter 4 – Numbers, Dates, Telling Time, and Formal Speech in French	24
Chapter 5 – Basic Grammar and Guidelines in Constructing French Sentences	36
Conclusion	44

Introduction

I want to thank you and congratulate you for downloading the book, *"Learn French"*.

This book contains helpful information about learning French, and how a beginner can learn the basics of this language fast!

You will discover the different grammar rules for when writing in French, as well as the rules associated with plural, neutral, feminine, and masculine versions of different words.

This book includes tips and techniques to help you learn French fast, including basic words and common phrases! You will learn how to count in French, understand the date and time, and learn common and useful sentences and words.

At the completion of this book you should have a good understanding of the French language, and the rules associated. All that will be left to do is increase your vocabulary until you consider yourself to be fluent!

Thanks again for downloading this book, I hope you enjoy it, and good luck!

Chapter 1 – An Introduction to the French language

For many people, learning another language other than what they are used to is a huge challenge. After all, they do not have the opportunity of starting with an empty vocabulary like they did as babies. However, this doesn't mean that becoming successful in this endeavor is impossible. And if ever you choose to learn a language, French may be the one that you consider studying.

This chapter will give a brief introduction about the French language along with some basics as to how the language can be learned easily.

What is French?

French is a part of the Romance languages, tracing its roots from Latin. It was developed because of the influence of the Celtic and Frankish people in Gaul (which is known today as France). Since it is a Romance language, it is related to many different languages such as Italian, Portuguese, Romanian, and Spanish. According to recent statistics, French is spoken by more than 87 million people as their native language along with almost 70 million people as non-native speakers. French is the official language of 29 countries. Even Canada, which is fairly close to the US, includes French as one of its official languages. In fact, producers of packaged consumer goods are required by the Canadian government to use both English and French on their labels!

How did French come into existence?

To better appreciate what the language is, it is also necessary to know of its brief history.

As mentioned, French gets its roots from Latin. This is because during the occupation of the Romans on Gaul, the natives of the territory were forced to learn Latin. Eventually, the natives developed what was known as Vulgar Latin, which is very similar to the mother language. Over the course of time, the language was heavily influenced by the Franks and the Celts, developing the *la langue d'oïl*. One of its dialects, the *le francien*, became the official language of the Kingdom of France.

Up until the 19th century, French became the dominant language all over Europe, and it was used in diplomacy, spreading culture, trading, and in the royal courts of different countries. This influence also extends to other languages, even English. In fact, a third of all the words in English are derived from French.

Why should you learn French?

You may be wondering that out of all the languages available for you to learn, why would you prioritize French?

One good reason why you would want to study French is because of the huge number of people who use it, whether the figures are referring to native speakers or not. This simply means that if ever you have plans to visit or move to another country which lists French as one of its official or spoken languages, it will be easier for you to communicate with the locals. The huge number of speakers around the world also makes it easier to learn; after all, learning the language is best if there is a native speaker to help guide you.

Another reason for doing so is that many materials are available in French – be it movies, novels, or non-fiction works. Obviously, you cannot always rely on translated documents as the meaning of the content may be lost. By understanding spoken and written French, you will be able to acquire more knowledge, or better appreciate French entertainment.

Learning a new language is also a way of learning and appreciating the culture of the country or place where it originated. This will give you a better insight into France and its people.

Lastly, learning French is a great exercise not only for your brain but also for your speaking skills. Unlike English, French is more diverse when it comes to the pronunciation of words. This will obviously be a challenge to the person's vocabulary, motivation, and ability to pronounce the words in a way that will make them sound like a native speaker.

How can French be learned easily?

For many people, French is a language that can be difficult to learn. However, there are things that can be done to make the learning of French easier:

- The most obvious technique to learn French at a much faster rate is to practice regularly. Unfortunately, language is one of the skills that can be "washed away" if it is not used on a regular basis. Even if you cannot practice everyday, just make sure that your French vocabulary and knowledge is revisited consistently.

- If possible, have somebody who knows the language assist you. This is mostly useful if you are trying to learn how to read and pronounce words, as well as if you would want to converse with another French speaker. If your companion came from a French-speaking country, it's highly possible that they know all the rules of their language by heart – and with their assistance, you will learn all there is to know about French.

- If you do not know someone who can speak the language, you can make use of the Internet as a way to learn it. Podcasts and videos are available so that you can learn about pronunciation, especially when it comes to difficult phrases, words, or even letters!

- Start with the pronunciation of the letters first. While French doesn't use characters to write their words (just like how it is in Japanese), it still features some letters that may have a different pronunciation or are not really used in your native language. Before you jump into learning about basic French phrases, it's necessary that you know how to properly pronounce first. Once you know the basics of French pronunciation, you can then move up to combining them and forming words, sentences, and eventually paragraphs.

Now that you've learned about the short history of the French language, identified your reasons for learning it, and kept in mind the tips to easily learn it, you can now advance to learning the basics of French grammar.

Chapter 2 – The French Alphabet, Accents, and Punctuation

Just like any other language, learning French starts with learning about its smallest components – the alphabet. This chapter will introduce the French alphabet, the rules on how they are pronounced, and the accents and punctuations commonly used in written French.

How to pronounce the alphabet?

French letters are no different from English letters, since the letters used by the latter are also used to by the French in writing. However, the difference between French and English lies in the pronunciation and the use of several accents.

The following will enumerate the non-accent letters used in the French alphabet and how each must be pronounced:

- Aa – pronounced as *ah*, as in f**a**ther

- Bb – pronounced as *bay*

- Cc – Generally, its French pronunciation is *say*. However, its pronunciation will change depending on the situation. If this letter comes before I and E, it must be pronounced as the English S (similar to how C in the word **c**enter is pronounced). If it comes before A, O, and U, its pronunciation must be the same as c in **c**at.

- Dd – pronounced as *day*, or similar to D in the word **d**og

- Ee – must sound like *euh*, similar to the emphasis of U in the word b**u**rp

- Ff – sounds like *eff*, similar to how F is pronounced in the word **f**og

- Gg – As a general rule, this letter is pronounced as *jhay*. However, its pronunciation will change depending on the word. If this letter is found before the vowels A, O, and U, it must sound like the g in the word **g**et. On the other hand, if it's placed before I and E, the pronunciation must be similar to the S in the word mea**s**ure.

- Hh – While this letter generally sounds as *ash* and is found in French written words, it is ALWAYS silent, even if the word begins with this letter. However, H has two kinds in the French language that are useful in writing. In non-aspirated H (or H muet), the letter H is treated as a vowel and the word requires either liaisons or contractions (other rules will be discussed in a later section). On the other hand, in an aspirated H (or H aspiré), the word is treated is a consonant and will not require liaisons or contractions. To determine which words are aspirated or not so that words can be spelled and pronounced correctly, French dictionaries place an asterisk (or any other symbol) on words starting with an H to indicate that they are aspirated.

- Ii – sounds like *ee*, or similar to how the letters *ea* in the word t**ea**m is pronounced

- Jj – pronounced as *ghee*, and sounds like the S in the word mea**s**ure

- Kk – sounds like *kah*, and is pronounced like the K in the word **k**ite

- Ll – a straightforward *el* pronunciation, similar to L in the word **l**emon

- Mm – simply pronounced as *emm*, from M in the word **m**inute

- Nn – similar to N in the word **n**ote, as it sounds like *enn*

- Oo – This letter can be pronounced as the O in the word n**o**se, or can also sound similar to the U in n**u**t.

- Pp – pronounced as *pay*, or similar to the letter P in the word **p**en

- Qq – sounds like *ku*, or how the K in kite is pronounced

- Rr – must sound like you're saying *air*. To do this correctly in French, you must try to force air as if it's going to the back of your throat. Your tongue must be near the position where you gargle, but the letter must sound softly.

- Ss – Generally, it must sound like *ess*. However, the pronunciation might change depending on the word. If the word begins with an S or has 2 S's, it must sound like the S in **sis**ter. However, if the word only has one S, it must sound like the Z in the word ama**z**ing.

- Tt – pronounced as *tay*, just like t in the word **t**op

- Uu – To pronounce this properly, you must say the letter E as how it is said in English while making sure that your lips follow the position like you're saying "*oo*".

- Vv – pronounced as *vay*, and sounds like the V in **v**iolin.

- Ww – pronounced as *dubla-vay* as the general rule. However, this may be changed depending on the word. It can sound like V in the word **v**iolin, or as W in the word **w**ater.

- Xx – sounds like *eeks,* and can be pronounced either like gz (as how the word e**x**it is said) or as ks (when the word socks is said).

- Yy – pronounced as *ee-grehk*, or similar to ea in l**ea**k.

- Zz – sounds as *zed,* or like the letter Z in **z**ebra.

The pronunciations indicated above are mostly used if you want to spell something out, such as your name. Using the French pronunciations for each alphabet will make things clearer if you are talking to someone who uses French. For example, if your name is Hilda and you want to spell it out, your companion will better understand it if you say *Ash-Ee-El-Day-Ah*.

Rules on final consonants

Another French rule that is not observed in English is that certain consonants are not pronounced (silent) when they are the final letters of the word. While having silent letters is not new in the English language (words such as psychology or psoriasis have silent P), this is not a very prominent rule as compared to the French grammar.

Some of the consonants that are usually silent when at the end of the word are the letters D (as *nord* or North), S (such as *cas* or case/event in English), P and T (such as in the word *coup d'état* or revolution), and X (such as in the word *paresseux* or lazy in English).

There are also some consonants that border on being pronounced in some words but are silent in others. Some of these "borderline" silent final consonants are the letters C (which is pronounced in the word *parc* or garden, but not in the word *blanc* or white), F (pronounced in the word *neuf* or new, but not in the word *nerf* or nerve), L (which is pronounced in *miel* or honey, but is not pronounced in the word *sourcil* or eyebrow), and R (where it is heard in the word *hier* or yesterday, but not in the word *premier* or first).

Rules on the dental consonants

Although the pronunciations of the letters in the French alphabet were tackled earlier, their pronunciations are not always applicable when the letters are combined to say the word. There are certain consonants which cannot be pronounced correctly if you only apply your knowledge of the English language.

In order to correctly pronounce the letters d, n, t, l, s, and z correctly in French, what you can do is to pronounce the letters in such a way that the tip of your tongue is on your lower teeth while the middle of your tongue is against the roof of your mouth. This is very different from what is done when the same letters are pronounced in English. By becoming conscious of your tongue's position while you're saying those letters, it will be easier for you to pronounce French words such as *voudrais* or even combine with a phrase such as *Je voudrais manger* (I'd like to eat).

Punctuation

Another important component in French, most especially with written materials, is the punctuations. Fortunately, most of the punctuations used in English have the same purpose in French.

This table will enumerate the commonly used punctuations used in French along with their French names:

Punctuation	English name	French name
{ }	Brackets	Accolades
'	Apostrophe	Apostrophe
@	At symbol	Arobase
*	Asterisk	Astérisque
\	Backslash	Barre oblique inverse
/	Slash	Barre oblique
[ ]	Hooks	Crochets
:	Colon	Deux points
#	Sharp or Number sign	Dièse
$	Dollar sign	Dollar
=	Equal sign	Égal
&	And	Esperluette
« »	Quotation marks	Guillemets
<	Less than	Inférieur à
>	Greater than	Supérieur à
-	Hyphen/Dash; Minus sign	Tiret; moins

( )	Parentheses	Parenthèses
+	Plus	Plus
.	Period	Point
!	Exclamation point	Point d' exclamation
?	Question mark	Point d' interrogation
%	Percent	Pourcent
;	Semi-colon	Point Virgule
_	Underscore	Soulignement
~	Tilde	Tilde
,	Comma	Virgule

French materials do not use the English quotation mark; instead, they use the unique guillemets (« »). However, the purpose of this punctuation is the same as the former.

Accents

Last on our discussion would be the accents. Although the accents are also used in the English language, words with such are not that common. However, accents are very useful in French mainly because the meaning of the words will change depending on whether an accent is present or not. For example, the French word *la* is equivalent to the English word "the". However, if the same word is spelled as *là* (wherein one letter was given a grave accent), its English equivalent becomes "there".

French words make use of five accents, which are the following:

Accent Name	Letters where the accent is used
Acute accent (*accent aigu*)	Letter Éé only
Cedilla (*cédille*)	Letter Çç only
Circumflex (*accent circonflexe*)	Used in all vowels (Ââ, Êê, Îî, Ôô, Ûû)
Diaeresis (*tréma*)	Used in Ëë, Ïï, Üü, and Ÿÿ
Grave accent (*accent grave*)	Letters Èè, Àà, and Ùù

Acute accent

This is the most commonly used accent in materials written in French, even though it is only used with the letter E. With the accent, the previous pronunciation of E is changed to *ay*.

One of the main uses of this accent is to change the form of regular –*er* verbs into its past principle. An example would be that the word *aimer* (which means "to love") can be changed to *aimé* and become its past principle (which means "loved").

Another function of the acute accent is that it helps people to translate certain French words into English. If the word to be translated starts with É, what you can do is to replace it with the letter S. While this is not true in all cases, there are instances wherein the substitution will give you an idea of the English equivalent for that French word. For example, if the French word *école* has its first letter substituted with S, you will end up with the word *scole*. If this is pronounced as an English word, it closely resembles the word school. True enough, *école* literally means school in English. This rough translation could be one reason as to why the acute accent is the most common in written French.

Cedilla

If you have tried to read French materials, there is a possibility that you have encountered words with a uniquely written letter C. In French, this is called as a *cédille*.

Fortunately, this is only encountered for the letter C. The only function of this accent is to make the letter's pronunciation softer, making it sound like an S. With the cedilla, one can be certain that the letter will be pronounced as such. This is also helpful if you encounter a word that does not fall in the category described earlier regarding how the letter must be pronounced.

Let's take a look at the French phrase *le garçon*, which is translated as "the boy" in English. Since C comes before the letter O, it must follow the rule stated earlier wherein the former's pronunciation must be the same as C in cat. However, because of the cedilla, it becomes clear to the reader that the letter's pronunciation must be the same as the letter S.

Circumflex

Another accent symbol used in French written materials is the circumflex, which is commonly attached to the vowels of the French alphabet. This accent has the following functions:

- The presence of the circumflex changes the pronunciation of the vowels a, e, and o. From the pronunciations mentioned above, their pronunciations are now changed to sound like a longer *ah* (for letter A), sounds like *ai* in the English word **fair** (for letter E), and is pronounced as *oh* (for letter O).

- Another function of the circumflex is that it can help readers to identify which word is being described. This is especially useful if the word being referred to has another word with the same sound and spelling but has a different meaning. For example, the French words *sur* and *sûr* have the same spelling. But because of the circumflex, it will be easier to identify that one word refers to the preposition "on" while the accented word refers to the adjective "sure".

Diaeresis

Also included in the study of accents is the diaeresis, which is distinguished by two points at the top of the letter.

The function of the diaeresis in the French language is that it helps people to identify that the part of the word where the accent is found must be pronounced as if it is a different word, helping the listener to understand what the word really means.

Let's take a look at the words *naïve* and *maïs*. These words, if written without the diaeresis, would be pronounced as "*neuhv*" and "*meh*" (because of the silent final consonant), respectively. These pronunciations will obviously make the word unrecognizable. However, with the diaeresis, the pronunciations of the word will be changed into "*ma.is*" and "*na.iv*", respectively. This will make it easier for the person to identify that the first word refers to corn, while the other is referred to an innocent person.

Grave accent

Last on our list of accents used in the French language is the grave accent. Just like the previously discussed symbols, the grave accent fulfills a specific function which depends on the letter where it is found.

If the accent is found in letters A and E, its purpose is to distinguish the meaning of one word from another. Aside from the example (*la* and *là*) in this section's introduction, the words *ou* and *où* will have a different meaning when the grave accent is present. The non-accented *ou* refers to the conjunction "or", while the *où* is referring to the word "where".

For words whose letter E has a grave accent, its function is more on the letter's pronunciation. Normally, an unaccented E has the same pronunciation as the English article "a", and can sometimes be omitted (not pronounced) if the word is said rapidly. But with the presence of the accent, the è of the word is now pronounced similar to the letter E in the word p**e**t.

With the knowledge of the French letters' pronunciation, the punctuations used in written materials, and knowing about the functions of each accent, studying the language further will not be that difficult. You should aim to become proficient in the elements discussed in this chapter so that it will be easier for you to learn how to read and write in French.

Chapter 3 – Liaisons and Contractions

Another important rule in the French language that revolves around pronunciation is the use of liaisons and contractions. While these concepts were introduced in the previous chapter during the discussion of letter H's pronunciation, these are not entirely tied to the latter.

This chapter will clarify what liaisons and contractions are as well as when these should be executed when writing and speaking.

What is a liaison?

If you already know the standard definition of this term, it will be easier to remember its meaning when placed in the context of French language.

If you can recall, it was mentioned in the previous section as the general rule for pronouncing French words is that if it ends in a consonant, that letter must not be pronounced. However, this is not always applicable in some cases. Not only can it confuse the listener as to the word being referred to by the speaker, it can also make the conversation sound awkward. If this happens in a conversation, what you can do is to apply liaisons – which is observed when the normally silent final consonant in a word is pronounced as if it is part of the word that is following it.

Rules surrounding liaison

The condition for using liaison is this: if the word ending in a silent consonant is followed by a word that starts with a vowel or a non-aspirated H, liaisons can be used.

To better understand this rule, take a look at the sample phrases below:

The French word *ont* (equivalent to the pronoun we or they) is pronounced as *on*. If this word is combined and becomes *ont-ils* (which translates to "have they"), the pronunciation then becomes "*on teel*". This is in compliance with the previously mentioned rule that the final consonant of the previous word is pronounced as if it's part of the next.

Along with this condition, the use of liaison may also require the person to change the pronunciation of the final consonant, depending on the word where liaison is used.

Take a look at this example:

The French phrase *vous avez*, in compliance with the previous rule, will have the final S of the word *vous* pronounced. However, what will happen is that rather than pronounce it to sound like S, it will be pronounced like the letter Z – meaning, the phrase will be pronounced as "*vu za vay*".

To know how the pronunciation of final consonants will be affected, take a look at this guide:

Letter	Must be pronounced as
D	T
F	V
S	Z
X	Z
G	G
N	N
P	P

R	R
T	T
Z	Z

Aside from the rules mentioned earlier, there are other specific rules surrounding the use of liaison, depending on the category that it is in – required, forbidden, and optional liaisons.

Required liaisons

As the name suggests, this requires the person to pronounce the words according to the rules surrounding liaisons. Required liaisons are usually observed on words that are syntactically related.

To get an idea as to when required liaisons are observed, it is important that the word falls under any of the guidelines listed below:

- If an adjective, article, or number is followed by an adjective or noun. For example, the French phrase *un homme* (a man) is composed of an article and a noun which starts with a non-aspirated H (treating it as a vowel) will be pronounced as *"uh nuhm"*. Another example would be *deux enfants* (two children), a combination of a number and a noun, which is now produced as *"deu zan fan"*.

- Any combination of pronoun and verb or adjective, verb and pronoun, and two pronouns also require liaisons. The previous examples *vous avez* and *ont-ils* fall on this category. Another example would be the phrase *nous en avons* (translated as "we have"), which is a combination of pronoun and verb. Its pronunciation will now become *"nu za na von"*.

- Certain single syllable conjunctions, prepositions, and adverbs may also be subject to required liaisons. For example, the phrase *tout entire* (whole), is an adverb and must be pronounced as *"tu tan tyay"*. Remember that not all words that fit in this category are subject to being pronounced with liaison.

- Many of the fixed expressions in French must be pronounced with liaison. Some of the common expressions where this rule is applied are *c'est-à-dire* (which means "that is to say", is pronounced as *"say ta deer"*), *comment allez-vous* (the English equivalent of "How are you?", and is pronounced as *"ko man ta lay vu"*), and *avant hier* (which means "the day before yesterday", is now pronounced as *"a van tyer"*).

Forbidden liaisons

This type of liaison is referred to as the combination of words wherein the final consonant of the first word must NEVER be pronounced along with the second word even if the latter starts with a vowel or a non-aspirated H. Words fall in this category if ever pronouncing it with the liaison will create confusion due to the similarity of the expression with another (but has a meaning different from what was intended).

The following will serve as a guideline to identify that the final consonant of the first word must not be pronounced:

- Liaison is forbidden if the affected words come after the singular noun. Take a look at the French phrase *un garçon intelligent*, which means "an intelligent boy" in English. In this sentence, the liaison occurs between the words *garçon* and *intelligent*. In this case, the phrase must be pronounced as *"gar son en te lee zha"*, wherein the letter N in *garçon* is not connected with the next word.

- No liaison must be pronounced if the affected word is found after names. Take a look at the phrase *Albert est parti,* which is translated as "Albert left". In this example, you can see that the word *est* comes after the name Albert. Thus, during pronunciation, this phrase must sound like *"al ber ay par tee"* in order to comply with this guideline.

- If the word comes after the French conjunction *et* (and), the liaison is also not mentioned as part of the second word. For example, in the phrase *un garçon et une fille* (which means "a boy and a girl"), it can be seen that the *une* is following *et*. To comply with the forbidden liaison rule, this phrase will be pronounced as *"un gar son ay un feey"*.

- If the final consonant of the first word is followed by an aspirated H word. Even though H aspiré words are to be treated as consonants, the fact that H is never pronounced in French somehow makes it sound like the second word is starting with a vowel. For example, the phrase *les heros* (the heroes) has the H aspire word *heros*. In order to avoid confusion, it is forbidden for the speaker to pronounce it with a liaison. If one attempts to do so, the phrase will sound as *"lay ze ro"* (complying with the change in the pronunciation for letter S) and will convey the message "zero" rather than "hero". For this example, the proper pronunciation is *"lay ay ro"*.

- If the target word is found before the French words *onze* (eleven) and *oui* (yes), its final consonant will not be mentioned. Take a look at the phrases *un oui et un non* (a yes and a no) and *les onze élèves* (eleven students). From these examples, it is evident that the words following them ends with a consonant, and must not be pronounced. Therefore, the pronunciations of these phrases must be *"lay on zay lev"* and *"un wee ay un non"*, respectively.

Optional liaison

The last on the categories of liaison would be the optional liaison. For this category, you can choose whether the words which fit the liaison category will be pronounced or not. Regardless of the decision, whether to pronounce or not, the meaning of the word will still be the same and the pronunciation will still be considered as correct.

In order to qualify if the words can be pronounced with or without liaison, take a look at the following guidelines:

- If the affected word is found after plural nouns, the liaison can either be pronounced or not. For example, in the phrase *livres utiles* (useful books), the first word is in its plural form. Since it fits for the liaison, you have an option to pronounce it as *"liv reu zu teel"*. But even if you follow the previous rule wherein the final consonant must not be pronounced (that is, you will be saying the phrase as *"li vru teel"*, it will still sound correct.

- Liaisons may or may not be pronounced if the affected word is found between two-part verbs. For example, the phrase *je suis allé* (which is translated as "I am going") can be pronounced as either *"swee za lay"* or *"swee a lay"*. Since no other meaning can be conveyed when the other pronunciation is made, any of the two can be used when conversing.

- You can choose to pronounce or not pronounce the liaison if the present tense of *être* is combined with another adjective, adverb, or noun. For example, the phrase *il est heureux* (which means "He is happy"), which is in its present be-form, can be pronounced as either *"ee lay teu reu"* (liaison pronounced) or *"ee lay eu reu"* (liaison not pronounced).

- If the adverb or preposition is composed of multiple syllables, liaison can be pronounced or not. An example would be the phrase *assez utile*, which is translated in English as "rather useful". Since the expression is multi-syllabic, both the pronunciations *"a say zu teel"* and *"a say u teel"* are correct.

Contractions

Another concept that will help you to learn French at a much faster rate would be to learn about contractions.

Just as what the name suggests, this concept refers to omitting certain letters and/or sounds so that the word can be shortened without changing its meaning. In English, it is not always necessary for them to contract the words. For example, you can use either the word "that is" or "that's", depending on whatever it is that you prefer. However, the French language requires the use of contractions in some of its words in order for the pronunciation (or even the meaning) to be easier and clearer.

To prove that using contractions are mandatory, let's take a look at the words "that is" and "that's" once again. While English speakers and writers can choose any of those forms when communicating, the French will only require the contracted form of these words. In French, the same phrase will only be written as *c'est* (that's), which came from the words *ce* (the) and *est* (is). Since the words will follow the "final consonant" rule, the pronunciation of the uncontracted word will be the same as when it is contracted. With the contraction, the pronunciation and the writing of the word will be easier.

Rules on contraction

Fortunately, some of the basic rules that should be kept in mind as to when contractions must be made are easy to remember.

One general rule in the use of contractions would be if the word is followed by a non-aspirated H, a vowel, or the pronoun *y* (there), the vowel of the previous word must be dropped and must be contracted to the next. This is applicable on words that start with the definite articles *le* and *la*. For example, the words *le usine* can be contracted so that it is spelled as *l'usine,* which refers to "factory". This can also be applied to words that only contain a single consonant and are ending with a non-pronounced E. Some of the words that fall under this category would be *te, se, ce, de, me, ne, je, le,* and *que*. Another example (aside from *c'est)* to better explain this concept would be combining the words *je* and *habite*. Combined with a non-aspirated H, the first word will be contracted and will now result into the word *j'habite,* which means "I live". Lastly, this rule must be applied when the conjunctions *lorsque* (which could mean as either when or during) and *puisque* (which can be translated into since or as) are included in the phrase. For example, if *puisque* is combined with the word *on,* it will result in *puisqu'on,* which specifically means as "since". Likewise, combining *lorsque* with *il* results in *lorsqu'il* and will have the specific meaning "when".

By studying these basic rules of the French language, you will have a solid base of reading and pronouncing French words and thus be able to convey the message clearly to your listener.

Chapter 4 – Numbers, Dates, Telling Time, and Formal Speech in French

In this chapter, the discussion will revolve on teaching you words which are commonly used in conversations – knowing how to say numbers, dates, time, and delivering greeting so that the conversation will have a formal register.

How to say numbers in French

While not all conversations involve the use of numbers, there are many situations they're used. For example, if you will be going to the market and will be asking for the price of the product, its use is unavoidable. Thus, you need to know the French equivalent of each number.

This table will serve as your guide in learning the French equivalent of numbers:

Number	French word	Number	French word
1	*Un*	14	*Quatorze*
2	*Deux*	15	*Quinze*
3	*Trois*	16	*Seize*
4	*Quatre*	17	*Dix-sept*
5	*Cinq*	18	*Dix-huit*
6	*Six*	19	*Dix-neuf*
7	*Sept*	20	*Vingt*
8	*Huit*	21	*Vingt et un*

9	Neuf	22 to 29	Vingt-[deux up to neuf]
10	Dix	30	Trente
11	Onze	31	Trente et un
12	Douze/ Une douzaine	32 to 39	Trente-[deux up to neuf]
13	Treize	40	Quarante
50	Cinquante	90	Quatre vingt dix
60	Soixante	91 to 99	Quatre vingt [onze up to dix neuf]
70	Soixante dix	100	Cent/ Une centaine (one hundred)
71	Soixante et onze	200 to 900	[Deuf up to neuf] cents
72 to 79	Soixante-[douze up to dix neuf]	201	Deux cent un
80	Quatre vingts	901	Neuf cent un
81	Quatre vingt un	1,000	Mille/ Un millier (one thousand)
82 to 89	Quatre vingt [deux up to neuf]	1,000,000	[Un] million

As you can see from the table above, the syntax followed by the numbers are quite different from the English mode of counting. In order to avoid confusion when it comes to translating numbers, you must first memorize the French equivalent from numbers 1 to 20. This is because the French have a different name for each of those numbers, and the pattern for the French equivalent doesn't start until 21.

Once the names for numbers 1 to 20 are memorized, another guideline that must be remembered is that by number 70, you will be using *soixante dix* (which are the terms for number 60 and 10, respectively), and its succeeding numbers will follow by the French equivalent for numbers 11 to 19. For number 80, whose French equivalent is *quatre vingts*, the idea is to multiply the 2 numbers. The pattern starts again by applying the French equivalents from 1 to 20, making the number 91 to follow the French equivalent for the numbers 11 to 19.

Lastly, remember the terms for the hundreds, thousands, and millions place. The same pattern from numbers 1 to 100 will be followed, with only the prefix for those places being changed and the term for the place always coming before the number. For example, if you will be referring to the number 125, its French equivalent will be *un cent deux cinq*.

Telling the date

Another area that may be present in a conversation would be dates. Obviously, the French do have their own equivalents for the days of the week, the months of a year, and other expressions that have something to do with the date.

Days of the week

The table below will guide you on the French names and proper pronunciation of each day in a week:

English term	French term	Pronunciation
Monday	*lundi*	*luhndee*
Tuesday	*mardi*	*mahrdee*
Wednesday	*mercredi*	*maircruhdee*
Thursday	*jeudi*	*juhdee*
Friday	*vendredi*	*vahndruhdee*
Saturday	*samedi*	*sahmdee*
Sunday	*dimanche*	*deemahnsh*

The French terms for each day of the week are not capitalized when written, which is the opposite of what is practiced in the English language.

In order to ask the question "What day is it today?" in French, there are three ways for how it can be delivered:

- *On est quel jour aujourd'hui?*
- *Quel jour sommes-nous aujourd'hui?*
- *Quel jour est-on aujourd'hui?*

All of these phrases have the same translation in English, even though each statement sounds different. The most common way of asking this question is the first, though this statement is usually less formal compared to the other two.

Another way for the same question to be asked even if the English equivalent is different would be *Aujourd'hui on est quel jour?* This French question can be translated as "Today is what day?" Fortunately, you can answer all of these questions with one French phrase, which is *Aujourd'hui on est [jour]*, which is translated in English as "Today is [the day]. Obviously, you only need to say the French equivalent of the day that you're referring to. For example, if today is a Sunday, you only replace the bracketed area with the French term, and your statement will be "*Aujourd'hui on est dimanche*".

Here are other phrases that might be helpful when engaged in conversations related to the day of the week:

French term	English equivalent
après-demain	After tomorrow or day after tomorrow
aujourd'hui	Today (may also be used if you are referring to the term "nowadays")
avant-hier	The day before yesterday
ce soir or *cette nuit*	Tonight
demain or *lendemain*	Tomorrow
dernière nuit	Last night
Hier	Yesterday (the French term may also be used to refer to "last night")

Months of the year

Upon knowing the French terms for each day of the week, it follows that you need to have knowledge of the more general area – in the case of telling the date, this refers to knowing the French translations for each month of the year.

This table will be your guide on the French equivalent of each month:

English term	French term	Pronunciation
January	*janvier*	*jzahnvyay*
February	*février*	*fayvryay*
March	*mars*	*mahrse*
April	*avril*	*ahvrill*
May	*mai*	*maye*
June	*juin*	*jzwan*
July	*juillet*	*jzuyay*
August	*août*	*oot* or *oo*
September	*septembre*	*septahmbruh*
October	*octobre*	*oktuhbr*
November	*novembre*	*novahmbr*
December	*décembre*	*daysahmbr*

Just like the days of the week, the French do not use capital letters when writing each month of the year.

If you would like to ask for the date (or would like to know if you are being asked of the date), remembering the French phrase *"Quelle est la date..."* is important. This phrase, which means "What is the date..." in English, can have an additional French term depending on the period that is being referred. For example, if you are asking another person of the date today, you will need to add the French equivalent for that specific day. In this particular situation, the French equivalent of the statement "What is the date today?" would be *"Quelle est la date d'aujourd'hui"*? Likewise, if you are asking for the date yesterday, you will only replace the term *d'aujourd'hui* with *d'hier*.

If you are to answer the question where you are asked for the date, the French statement would be *"C'est le [the date] [month]"*. While the order is reversed, this is translated as "It's [month] [date]. Obviously, you will be referring to the French equivalent of the numbers. For example, if you would like to answer that today is May 10, what you need to say in French is *"C'est le [dix] [mai]"*.

If ever you would want to refer to seasons (or *saison* in French), there are also French equivalents for each term. *Le printemps, l'été, l'automne,* and *l'hiver* can be translated as spring, summer, autumn, and winter, respectively.

Telling time

If encountering questions related to dates are to be expected, all the more that you need to expect that you'll be asked (or you will ask) about the time.

If you would like to ask for the time, the French phrases that you need to remember are *"Quelle heure il est?"* or *"Quelle heure est-il?"* These phrases both translate to the English phrase "What time is it?" Likewise, if you are the one being asked for the time, your sentence must be *"Il est [nombre] heures"*, or is translated as "It is [number] hours."

One important guideline when it comes to the French telling time would be the use of the word *heures*. While English speaking countries do understand even if you only say the number (for example, "It's ten"), this is not possible if you're talking to those who speak French. When it comes to writing time in French, they are used to the 24 hour system rather than adding the abbreviations AM and PM. Therefore, if you encounter French written materials, you will most likely see 16h30 or other similar formats to refer to 4:30 PM.

If you are telling time, you need to start the sentence with the French terms *"Il est"*. While this is literally translated as "he is", it can also be equivalent to "it is". This is important if you want to distinguish between time and date, because another French term, which is *c'est,* also means "it is".

Here are some sample statements that you can use as your reference when it comes to telling time:

English statement	**French equivalent**
What time is it?	*Quelle heure il est?* *Quelle heure est-il?*
It is one o'clock	*Il est une heure*
It is five o'clock	*Il est cinq heures*
It is ten o'clock	*Il est dix hures*
It is five (minutes) past ten o'clock	*Il est de cinq dix heures*
It is a quarter past ten o'clock	*Il est un quart de dix heures*
It is ten fifteen	*Il est dix heures quinze*
It is half past ten o'clock	*Il est dix heures et demie*
It is ten thirty	*Il est dix heures trente*
It is ten forty	*Il est dix heures quarante*
It is twenty to eleven	*Il est onze heures moins vingt*
It is a quarter till eleven/ It is ten forty-five	*Il est onze heures moins quart*
It is noon	*Il est midi*
It is midnight	*Il est minuit*

As you can see in the translations mentioned above, knowledge of numbers is necessary so that you will be able to tell time accurately. There are also two French translations even if the thought of the sentence is the same. For example, the statements "It is ten forty" and "It is twenty to eleven" have the same meaning but have different translations, depending on what message you would want to convey. For the first statement, it only used your knowledge in using the French translations for numbers. However, in the second statement (*Il est onze heures moins vingt*), the French translation requires some spinning on the syntax as well as using other words. If you translate the said French statement in literal English, it would mean "It is eleven o'clock minus twenty". Use whatever French translation is comfortable for you, and use the table above as your "stems" whenever you want to tell what time it is.

Other statements that may be useful in conversing but entails the use of relative time periods are found in the table below:

English term	French translation
A.M. or ...of the morning	...*du matin* (added to the sentence)
P.M. or ...of the evening	...*du soir*
Yesterday morning	*hier martin*
Afternoon	*l'après-midi*
Night	*la nuit*
Sunset	*le coucher du soleil*
Daybreak	*le lever du jour*
Sunrise	*le lever du soleil*
Morning	*le matin*

Noon or mid-day	*le midi*
Evening or In the evening	*le soir*
Rising sun	*le soleil levant*

Formal speech

In French, the use of certain words helps identify if the conversation is formal or not. Evidence to this fact is that unlike those who speak English, French speakers have a formal and informal version of the word "you" – and depending on which term is used, it will distinguish the conversation as formal or informal.

The difference between "vous" and "tu"

As mentioned, it is important to know where to use the right term so that the conversation will be formal. In French, this is depicted by the use of the words *vous* and *tu*.

The French term *vous* is the plural form of the pronoun "you", and can also be equivalent to other English pronouns such as "you guys", "all of you", and "you all". This term is used when addressing your friends or even if you are addressing a group of people. It is also used if you are talking to another person who is considered important (such as an authority figure or government officer), a person who is older than you, or even to somebody whom you are not familiar with. The use of *vous*, which is referred to as vouvoiement, is done in order to show respect, neutrality, or politeness to another person. This simply means that when *vous* is used, the conversation becomes formal.

On the other hand, the French term *tu* is the singular and more informal form of the word *vous*. The term is mostly used if you are talking to a family member, a friend, or when you are talking to children. Because the mood conveyed by the speech is informal, using it when talking to a stranger is considered as a sign of disrespect. As a general rule, the only time that you can use *tu* is if you are calling a person by his/her first name; if not, then you have to use *vous*.

The table below enumerates some of the terms that will further convey courtesy whenever you converse with another person:

English term	**French equivalent**
Thank You (very much/so much)	*Merci (beaucoup)*
You're welcome	*De rien* (literally translated as "not at all") *Pas de quoi* (can also be translated as "It's nothing") *Je vous en prie*
Please	*s'il vous plait* (literally translated as "If it pleases you") *s'il te plaît*

Another way of showing respect to other people is to address them using the correct titles. This table will enumerate the French equivalents for formal titles used when conversing or referring to another person:

Number	English term	French equivalent	French Abbreviation	Pronunciation
Singular	Ma'am or Mrs.	*Madame*	Mme	*mahdamn*
Plural	Ladies	*Mesdames*		*maydahm*
Singular	Miss or Young lady	*Mademoiselle*	Mlle	*mahdmwahzell*
Plural	Young ladies	*Mesdemoiselles*		*mehdmwahzell*
Singular	Mister or Sir	*Monsieur*	M.	*muhsyeu*
Plural	Gentlemen	*Messieurs*		*mehsyeu*

As a general rule, it is expected that one use the titles *madame, mademoiselle,* or *monsieur* when addressing someone who is older or people who are regarded as authority figures such as an employer or a professor. These terms may also be used alone, even if the last name of the person whom you're referring to is not mentioned. Therefore, even if you only address the person as such, the conversation is still considered formal.

Honing your French vocabulary is the key if you want to be able to converse more often using the French language. This is especially true if you will be engaged in the most common situations such as going to the supermarket, answering questions related to time and date, and addressing another person in a polite manner.

Chapter 5 – Basic Grammar and Guidelines in Constructing French Sentences

Learning about the French language is more than memorizing lines and responses. Once you have the knowledge of pronouncing the alphabet and have learned the French equivalent of the words that you would want to say, it is time to arrange them systematically so that your message can be conveyed in a way that the listener can easily understand. This is where the knowledge of French grammar comes in.

This chapter will discuss the important grammar points that beginning French speakers must remember.

Guidelines in converting a French noun into plural form

The general rule when creating plural nouns in French involves either adding an *–s* or *–x* or replacing the suffix *–al* with *–aux*. This rule obviously does not apply in making family names or words that end in *–s, -z,* and *–x* in their plural forms.

Here are some points that must be remembered if you want to turn a French singular noun into its plural form:

- In most cases, it is enough to simply add *–s* at the end of the word to make it plural. One example would be the French word *fleur*, which means "flower" in English. By applying this rule, converting *fleur* into *fleurs* automatically makes it plural. Another example would be the French word *chaise*, which is translated as "chair" in English. By simply adding –s, the word *chaises* now stands for "chairs".

- If the French noun ends in –*au*, the word can be converted into its plural form by placing an additional –*x*. One example would be the word *tableau*, which is the French translation for "table". To make it plural, you simply have to add –*x*; this will make the word's plural form as *tableaux*. Another example would be the French word *manteau*, which means "overcoat" in English. Following the rule, the word now becomes *manteaux*.

- If a French noun is ending with –*ou*, this is usually converted into plural by adding an –*s*. However, there are some words that end in –*ou* but can only be converted into its plural form by replacing it with –*x*. An example of a French word that falls in this category is *bijou* (translated as jewel), which becomes *bijoux* when converted into its plural form. Another would be *chou* (meaning cabbage), which is changed into *choux* when its plural form is required.

- If a French word is ending in –*al*, the only way to convert it to its plural form is to replace the previous suffix with –*aux*. For example, the French word *animal* (which also stands for "animal" in English) can only be converted to plural by replacing its previous suffix, making it *animaux*. Another example would be the word *journal* (the French term for "newspaper"). If this word is turned into its plural form, it will become *journaux*.

- If the French singular noun is ending in –*s, -z,* and –*x* but must be converted into its plural form, no changes are made on the last letter(s). For the change of the noun's form to become apparent, what you need to do is to simply change the article that is accompanying the word. Take a look at the phrase *un virus*, which is translated in English as "a virus". In French grammar, this word can be made into plural by changing the French article *un*. Therefore, its plural form would be *des virus*. Another example would be the French phrase *un Français*, which is translated as "A French" in English. Similar to the previous example, the noun will be unchanged – only the article. For this particular example, it can be in its plural form by using the word *les Francais*, which is translated "the French" or "French people".

- Unlike English, family names cannot be pluralized in French by adding the previous suffixes that make most nouns plural. If you are referring to a group of people who are in the same family, you will only need to add or change the accompanying article to its plural form. For example, if you are referring to "the Smiths", its French translation would be "les Smith" rather than add an *–s* to the surname.

How to match French adjectives to the nouns being described

Another basic component of any sentence would be the adjective, which is used to describe the noun. French grammar though, has a different guideline involving adjectives. This is because French adjectives need to reflect the gender and the number (either singular or plural) of the noun to be modified. The guidelines surrounding the use of adjectives are as follows:

- All nouns in French require a gender, which can either be masculine or feminine. Obviously, if the noun being described belongs to one of the genders, the adjective used in describing it must also belong to that gender. To know if the noun is grammatically male or female, you can look at the endings of the word. If the noun ends with *–age, -r, -t,* or *–isme,* it is most likely masculine. On the other hand, French nouns that end in *–ie, -ion, -ite or –ité, -nce,* and any of the *–nne, -mme,* and *–lle* extensions are feminine. Upon identifying the gender, you can now modify the adjective so that it will match the noun's gender.

- French nouns also require a number, which is either singular or plural. Regardless of the noun's gender, the adjective must match the number that it has.

How to change masculine singular adjective into feminine singular

In order to change the gender of a singular adjective, follow the guidelines mentioned below:

- The most common method of changing an adjective that has a masculine singular form into feminine singular would be to add an *–e* to the adjective. If you are consulting a French dictionary and encounter words that have the same meaning but one of them has *–e* at the end, this simply means that that adjective is a feminine singular. For example, the French adjective *noir* (black) can have the feminine gender by simply modifying its spelling to *noire*.

- If a masculine singular adjective is already ending with an *–e,* the abovementioned rule is not applicable. The spelling of the noun referred to remains as it is, as that word can be considered as either feminine or masculine. Some French adjectives that follow this rule are *utile* (useful), *calme* (calm), and *aimable* (nice).

- If the French adjective is ending with a vowel followed by a consonant, it can be made into a female singular by doubling the consonant first before placing an additional *–e*. One adjective that follow this guideline would be *mignon* (which means "cute"), which can be changed into its female singular form when it is spelled as *mignonne*. Another example would the French word *bon*, which is translated as "good" in English. Following the abovementioned rule, its female singular form is *bonne*.

- A general rule for most adjectives that end in *–eux* or *–eur* is to replace those suffixes with *–euse* to make it feminine singular. One French term that was also adapted in the English language and follows this rule would be the word *masseur*. This term, which is referring to a professional male massager, can have its gender changed easily by simply dropping the suffix *–eur* and use *–euse*. Thus, a female massager is referred to as *masseuse*. Another example would be the French adjective *heureux*, which is translated as "fat". To change its gender to feminine, change the said adjective to *heureuse*.

- If an adjective is ending with the suffix *–teur*, simply changing it into *–trice* automatically changes the word into its feminine singular form. For example, the French words *protecteur* (which means "protective") and *conservateur* (conservative) can simply be changed into their feminine singular forms when they are written as *protectice* and *conservatice*, respectively.

- Adjectives that are ending in *–er* can have their grammatical gender changed by replacing it with *–ère*. Some French adjectives that follow this rule are *premier* (which means "first"), *dernier* (which means "last"), and *cher* (which means expensive). When this rule is applied, the abovementioned words will become *première, dernière,* and *chère,* respectively.

- Most French adjectives that are ending in *–et* can be converted to their feminine singular forms by replacing the mentioned suffix with *–ète*. Some of the adjectives that comply with this rule are *complet* (translated as complete), *discret* ("discreet" in English), and *secret* (the same in English). Applying this rule, these terms will now become *complète, discrete,* and *secrète.*

- If the adjective is referring to the nationality and is ending with *–ain,* the rule is to simply add *–e* and not follow the previously mentioned rule regarding a vowel followed by a consonant. Some examples that follow this rule would be the *Mexicain* (referring to Mexicans) and *Américain* (referring to Americans). If these French adjectives are to be changed to their female singular forms, you will get *Mexicaine* and *Américaine,* respectively.

While the guidelines mentioned below will help you in converting almost any French adjective into its feminine form, there are other terms which do not follow any of the rules mentioned above. Some of the most common adjectives that have an irregular form when its gender is changed are as follows:

English adjective	French masculine singular form	French feminine singular form
Handsome or beautiful	*Beau*	*belle*
White	*Blanc*	*blanche*
Untrue/ False	*Faux*	*fausse*
New	*Nouveau*	*nouvelle*
Old	*Vieux*	*vieille*

Changing singular adjectives into plural

Since the adjective must also comply with the number that is attributed to your noun, you need to know how to make singular adjectives into plural form. These guidelines will help you in doing this:

- The most common way for making adjectives plural is to simply add an –s to the adjective, regardless of whether it is masculine or feminine. Let's take a look at the French adjective *vert*, which is translated as "green". If this adjective is converted into the female gender, it becomes *verte*. To make these terms plural, you simply add –s at the end, making them *verts* (for masculine) and *vertes* (for feminine).

- If the adjective already ends with an –s or an -x, there will be no need to place an additional –s to make it plural. Rather, the adjective remains the same and can be considered as both singular and plural. Some of the French adjectives that follow this category are *curieux* (translated as "curious"), *épais* (which means "thick"), and *gris* (translated as "gray").

- If the word is ending with an *–al*, simply drop the said adjective and replace it with *–aux* for it to become plural. For example, the French adjective *normal* can be converted into *normaux* so as to have a plural form.

- If the masculine singular adjective is ending with *–eau*, add an *–s* instead of *–x* to make it plural. For example, *nouveau* can be changed into *nouveaux*.

Once you have learned or became familiar with the basic grammar rules mentioned in this section, it will be easier for you to form sentences that are grammatically correct and will help you convey the message correctly.

Conclusion

Thank you again for downloading this book!

I hope this book was able to help you learn more about how to speak French!

The next step is to continually practice and add new words to your vocabulary. Once you have mastered the rules explained in this book, you simply need to increase the number of words that you know!

Finally, if you enjoyed this book, please take the time to share your thoughts and post a review on Amazon. It'd be greatly appreciated!

Thank you and good luck!

www.ingramcontent.com/pod-product-compliance
Lightning Source LLC
LaVergne TN
LVHW021740060526
838200LV00052B/3390